The Life Cycle of Bees

by Carol Pugliano-Martin

Table of Contents

Introduction 2
Chapter 1 How Do Bees Begin? 4
Chapter 2 What Bees Live in the Hive? 10
Chapter 3 What Happens to the Queen Bee? 14
Summary 20
Glossary 22
Index 24

Introduction

All living things have life **cycles**. Bees have a life cycle. Read to learn about bees.

Words to Know

cocoons

cycles

hatch

hives

larvae

pupae

queen bee

swarm

▲ These bees are living.

See the Glossary on page 22.

Chapter 1

How Do Bees Begin?

All bees begin as eggs.

▲ Bees begin as eggs.

Solve This

Bee eggs are 1.2 millimeters long. A pencil point is 1 millimeter long. Which is longer?

Answer: Bee eggs are longer.

Bees live in **hives**. The eggs are in the hive.

▲ This hive is in a tree.

▲ Eggs are in this hive.

Chapter 1

Larvae come from the eggs. Larvae **hatch** from the eggs. Larvae are baby bees.

▲ Larvae come from eggs.

It's a Fact

Bee eggs hatch in three days.

How Do Bees Begin?

Adult bees feed the larvae. The larvae grow.

▲ **Larvae eat. Larvae grow.**

Chapter 1

Larvae spin **cocoons**. Larvae use silk threads to spin cocoons. Cocoons protect larvae. Adult bees cover cocoons with wax.

▲ The larvae are in cocoons.

How Do Bees Begin?

The larvae are **pupae** now. Pupae last a few weeks. Then young bees come out.

▲ A young bee comes out.

Try This

Make a pupae.
1. Look at the photo of the cocoon.
2. Pretend an eraser is a bee.
3. Wrap string around the eraser to make a cocoon.
4. Cover the cocoon with clay.

Chapter 2

What Bees Live in the Hive?

Every hive has one **queen bee**. The queen bee lays the eggs. Queen bees lay many eggs.

▲ **Queen bees lay eggs.**

Queen bees are the biggest bees. All other bees are smaller.

▲ Queen bees are big.

Chapter 2

Smaller bees live in the hive. Some bees feed the queen bee.

▲ Bees feed the queen bee.

What Bees Live in the Hive?

Some bees clean the queen bee. The bees protect the queen bee. Bees work together in the hive.

It's a Fact

Worker bees live in the hive. Worker bees clean the queen bee. Worker bees feed the queen bee.

▲ Some bees help the queen bee.

Chapter 3

What Happens to the Queen Bee?

Some hives have too many bees. Then the queen bee leaves. Other bees leave, too.

▲ Some bees leave the hive.

It's a Fact

A new queen hatches in the hive.

The bees stay close together. The bees **swarm**.

▲ The bees stay together.

Chapter 3

The bees find a new home. Some bees make hives in trees.

▲ This hive is in a tree.

What Happens to the Queen Bee?

The queen bee lays more eggs.

▲ The queen lays eggs.

Chapter 3

Larvae hatch from the eggs. The larvae become pupae. Pupae become young bees.

▲ These pupae are in cocoons.

What Happens to the Queen Bee?

Queen bees live about four years. Then a new queen bee hatches. The life cycle of bees continues.

▲ **Queen bees live about four years.**

Summary

Bees have a life cycle. Bees hatch from eggs. Larvae become pupae. Pupae become young bees. New hives begin.

The Life Cycle of Bees

How Do Bees Begin?
- as eggs
- in hives
- larvae hatch
- adults feed larvae
- larvae grow
- larvae spin cocoons
- adults cover cocoons with wax
- become pupae
- young bees come out of pupae

What Bees Live in the Hive?
- the queen bee
- smaller bees
- bees that feed the queen bee
- bees that clean the queen bee
- bees that protect the queen bee

What Happens to the Queen Bee?

- queen bee leaves
- bees swarm
- finds a new home
- lays more eggs
- lives about four years
- new queen hatches

Think About It

1. How do bees begin?
2. What bees live in hives?
3. How do new hives begin?

Glossary

cocoons silk bags that larvae spin

*Larvae spin **cocoons**.*

cycles repeated circles of events

*All living things have life **cycles**.*

hatch come out of an egg

*Larvae **hatch** from the eggs.*

hives homes for bees

*Bees live in **hives**.*

larvae small creatures that become bees

Larvae come from the eggs.

pupae larvae in cocoons

Pupae last a few weeks.

queen bee the bee that lays eggs

*Every hive has one **queen bee**.*

swarm to move in a group

*The bees **swarm**.*

Index

adult bees, 7–8
baby bees, 6
bees, 2, 4–20
cocoons, 8
cycles, 2, 19–20
eggs, 4–6, 10, 17–18
hatch, 6, 18–20
hives, 5, 10, 12–14, 16, 20
larvae, 6–9, 18, 20
pupae, 9, 18, 20
queen bee, 10–14, 17, 19
swarm, 15
trees, 16
young bees, 9, 18, 20